NAPLAN NUMERACY SKILLS

Practice Test Book

NAPLAN Mathematics

Year 5

ISBN 978-1-925783-19-3

CONTENTS

INTRODUCTION
For Parents, Teachers, and Tutors

This book will provide thorough practice and complete preparation for the NAPLAN Numeracy tests. The first section contains practice sets to introduce students to the types of questions on the test. The second section contains three complete full-length practice tests just like the real NAPLAN Numeracy tests.

About the NAPLAN Numeracy Tests

The NAPLAN Numeracy tests assess whether students have the skills described in the Australian Curriculum. The mathematics curriculum covers the following three areas:

- Number and Algebra
- Measurement and Geometry
- Statistics and Probability

On the test, students answer around 40 questions covering all the skills described in the curriculum. While the majority of the questions are multiple-choice, others require students to provide a short written answer.

Introductory Practice Sets

The first section contains 3 shorter practice sets. These are similar to those found on the NAPLAN tests, but have 20 questions each. These introductory practice sets will allow students to become familiar with assessment questions before moving on to longer tests. These are perfect for warm-up activities and for providing feedback and guidance before students complete the full-length tests in the final section.

Complete Practice Tests

The second section contains three complete full-length practice tests just like the real NAPLAN Numeracy tests. Students will answer multiple-choice and short answer questions that cover all the skills assessed on the real test.

By completing these practice tests, students will have ongoing practice with assessment items, develop the mathematics skills they need, gain experience with all types of test questions, and be fully prepared for the NAPLAN Numeracy tests.

NAPLAN Mathematics

Year 5

Practice Set 1

Instructions

Read each question carefully. For each multiple-choice question, fill in the circle for the correct answer. For other types of questions, follow the directions given in the question.

1 Malcolm surveyed some people to find out how many pets they owned. The dot plot shows the results of the survey.

Number of Pets

	X			
X	X			
X	X			
X	X	X		
X	X	X	X	X
X	X	X	X	X
0	1	2	3	4

How many people owned 2 or more pets? Write your answer on the line below.

____

2 A square garden has side lengths of 8 inches. Jackie makes a rectangular garden with the same area as the square garden. Which of these could be the dimensions of the rectangular garden?

Ⓐ 10 inches by 6 inches

Ⓑ 7 inches by 9 inches

Ⓒ 8 inches by 12 inches

Ⓓ 16 inches by 4 inches

3 What is the measure of the angle below?

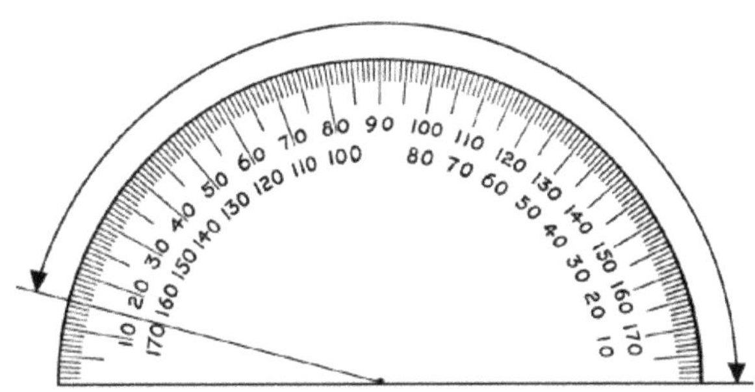

Ⓐ 15°

Ⓑ 25°

Ⓒ 165°

Ⓓ 175°

4 Camille cooked a cake on high for $1\frac{1}{4}$ hours. She then cooked it for another $\frac{1}{2}$ hour on low. Which diagram represents how long she cooked the cake for in all?

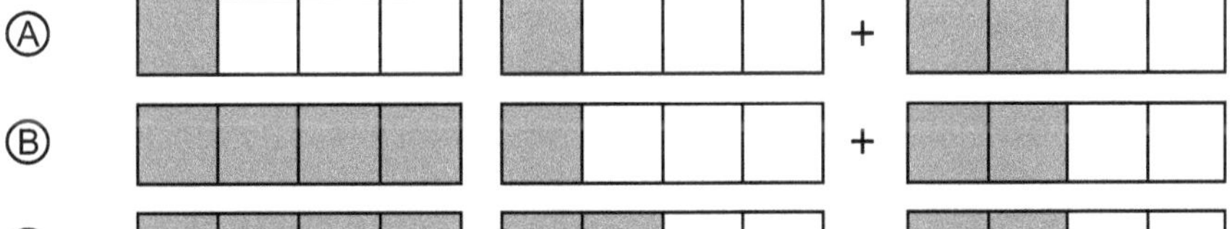

5 Which number makes the number sentence below true? Write the correct number in the box.

$$48 \div \square = 24$$

6 Which term describes the change shown below?

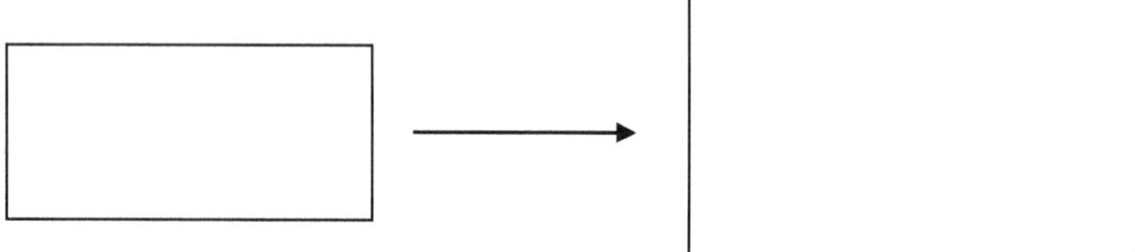

Ⓐ Rotation

Ⓑ Dilation

Ⓒ Translation

Ⓓ Reflection

7 Which fraction is the greatest?

Ⓐ $\frac{7}{10}$

Ⓑ $\frac{4}{5}$

Ⓒ $\frac{1}{5}$

Ⓓ $\frac{9}{10}$

8 The model below was made with 1-unit cubes.

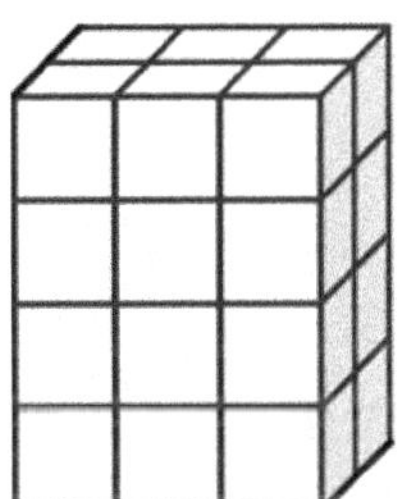

What is the volume of the model? Write your answer on the line below.

____________________ cubic units

9 An array for the number 36 is shown below.

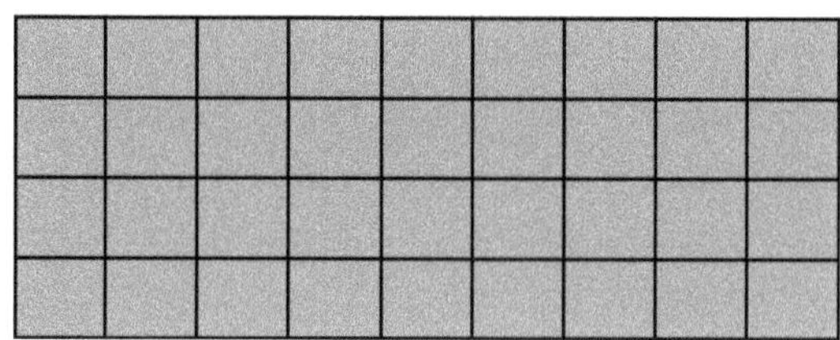

Which number is a factor of 36?

Ⓐ 5

Ⓑ 7

Ⓒ 8

Ⓓ 9

10 The table shows the amount of rainfall for the first four days of May.

Date	1st	2nd	3rd	4th
Rainfall (cm)	4.59	4.43	4.50	4.61

Which day had the lowest rainfall?

Ⓐ 1st

Ⓑ 2nd

Ⓒ 3rd

Ⓓ 4th

11 Sam kept a record of the types of movies each customer in his store rented. Sam made the frequency table below to show the results.

Type of Movie	Number of Rentals
Action	𝍸 𝍸 ||
Comedy	𝍸 𝍸 ||||
Drama	𝍸 𝍸 𝍸 |
Science fiction	𝍸 |||

What fraction of the movies rented were comedies?

Ⓐ $\frac{1}{4}$

Ⓑ $\frac{7}{50}$

Ⓒ $\frac{7}{25}$

Ⓓ $\frac{12}{43}$

12 The table shows the best times for running 100 metres of four students on the track team.

Student	Best Time (seconds)
Ramon	12.77
Ellis	12.63
Xavier	12.75
Colin	12.68

If each time is rounded to the nearest tenth, which student would have a best time of 12.7 seconds?

Ⓐ Ramon

Ⓑ Ellis

Ⓒ Xavier

Ⓓ Colin

13 Greg's volleyball team returns $\frac{4}{5}$ of the serves. Which of these shows how to represent the amount of serves returned as a decimal?

Ⓐ 0.4

Ⓑ 0.45

Ⓒ 0.6

Ⓓ 0.8

14 Mrs. Williams is preparing lemonade for a birthday party. She wants each child to have exactly 2 cups of lemonade with no lemonade left over. She needs to use 4 lemons to make each cup of lemonade. How many lemons will she need to make enough lemonade for 12 children? Write your answer on the line below.

____

15 Which single transformation is represented below?

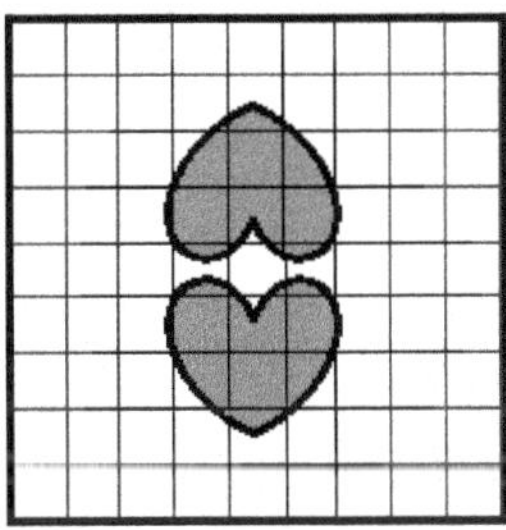

Ⓐ Reflection

Ⓑ Translation

Ⓒ Rotation

Ⓓ Dilation

16 Carmen tossed a coin 10 times. The coin landed on heads 6 times and tails 4 times. She wants to complete the tally chart below to show the results.

Heads	Tails

Which of these should Carmen place in the "Heads" column?

Ⓐ | | | |

Ⓑ 𝍸

Ⓒ 𝍸 |

Ⓓ 𝍸 | |

17 Lisa filled the box below with 1-centimetre cubes. How many 1-centimetre cubes would it take to fill the box?

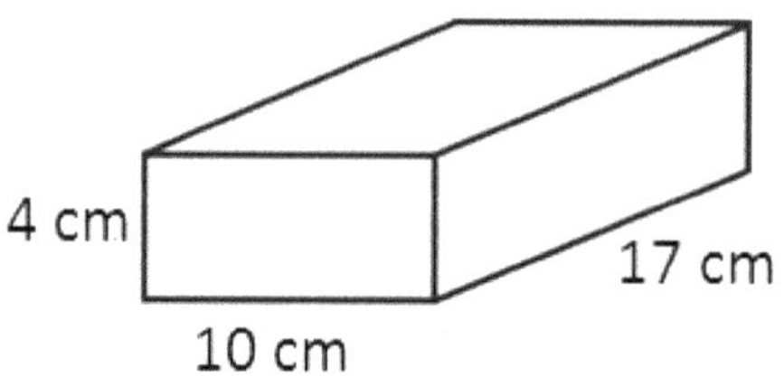

Write your answer on the line below.

____

18 Which of the following shows the shape of the base of the square pyramid below?

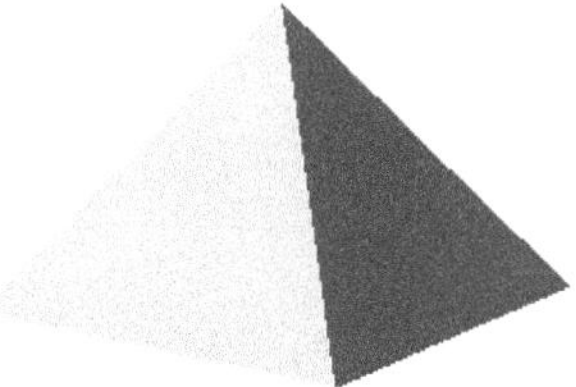

Ⓐ 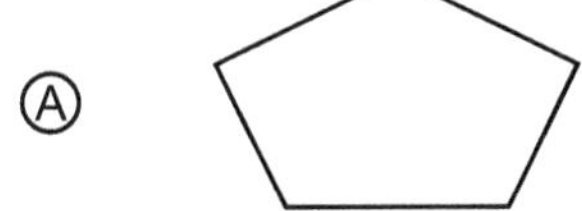

Ⓑ 

Ⓒ 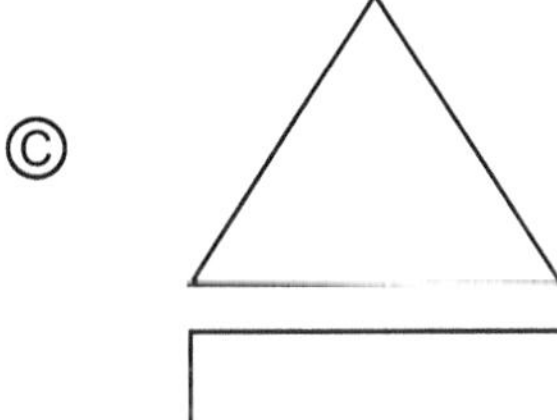

Ⓓ 

19 Lloyd has 4 white shirts and 1 blue shirt. He chooses one shirt at random. What is the probability he chooses a blue shirt?

Ⓐ 0.2

Ⓑ 0.25

Ⓒ 0.5

Ⓓ 0.8

20 Dominic received an invoice for a computer with a base price of $800, plus GST. The GST amount is 10% of the base price. What is the GST amount?

Ⓐ $8

Ⓑ $80

Ⓒ $808

Ⓓ $880

END OF PRACTICE SET

NAPLAN Mathematics

Year 5

Practice Set 2

Instructions

Read each question carefully. For each multiple-choice question, fill in the circle for the correct answer. For other types of questions, follow the directions given in the question.

1 The picture below represents a playground.

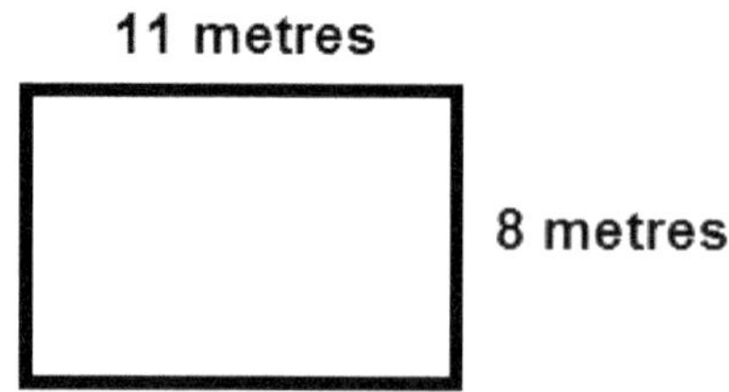

A fence is being built to go around the edge of the playground. The timber for the fence costs $14 per metre. If enough timber is bought to fit exactly around the edge of the playground, what will the total cost of the materials be? Write your answer on the line below.

$ ____________________

2 What is the perimeter of the rectangle below?

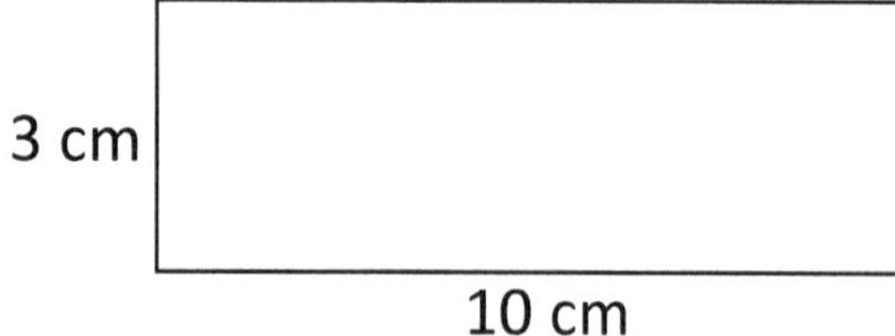

Ⓐ 13 cm

Ⓑ 30 cm

Ⓒ 26 cm

Ⓓ 60 cm

3 Jackie made this table to show how much she received in tips on the four days that she worked.

Day	Amount
Monday	\$32.55
Tuesday	\$31.98
Thursday	\$30.75
Friday	\$32.09

On which day did Jackie earn the most in tips?

Ⓐ Monday

Ⓑ Tuesday

Ⓒ Thursday

Ⓓ Friday

4 Which of these is equivalent to the time 19:00?

Ⓐ 7:00 a.m.

Ⓑ 7:00 p.m.

Ⓒ 9:00 a.m.

Ⓓ 9:00 p.m.

5 What is the volume of the model below?

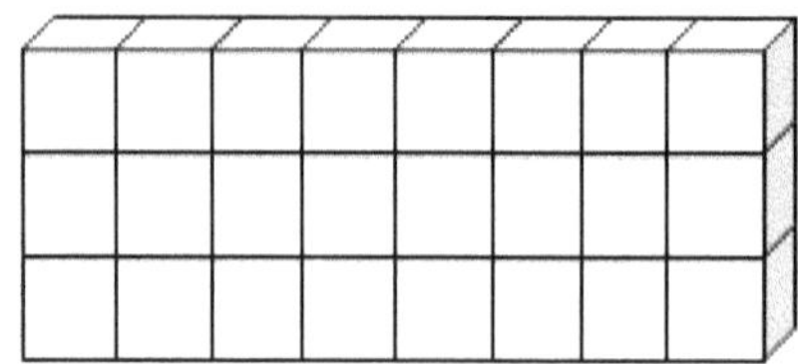

Write your answer on the line below.

____________________ cubic units

6 Zane folded the net shown below to form a shape.

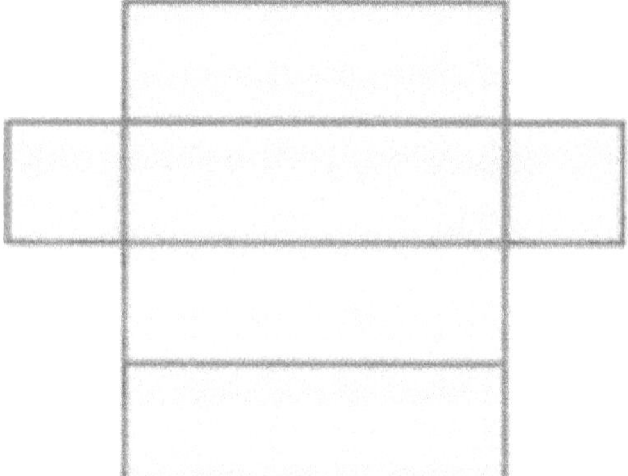

Which shape would Zane form?

Ⓐ Cube

Ⓑ Triangular prism

Ⓒ Rectangular prism

Ⓓ Square pyramid

7 A factory can fill 200 bottles of juice each hour. How many bottles of juice can be filled in each 12-hour shift? Write your answer on the line below.

____

8 A pattern has the rule $y = 2x + 4$. What is the value of y when $x = 5$?

Ⓐ 11

Ⓑ 14

Ⓒ 18

Ⓓ 30

9 The table shows the number of blocks of each colour in a bag.

Colour	Number
Red	12
Green	8
Yellow	16
Blue	4

Kathy selects a block at random. Which colour block has a 3 in 10 chance of being selected?

Ⓐ Red

Ⓑ Green

Ⓒ Yellow

Ⓓ Blue

10 Leo measures the length, width, and height of a block. He multiplies the length, width, and height. What is Leo finding?

Ⓐ Surface area

Ⓑ Mass

Ⓒ Volume

Ⓓ Perimeter

11 A farmer sells eggs in cartons of 6 eggs each.

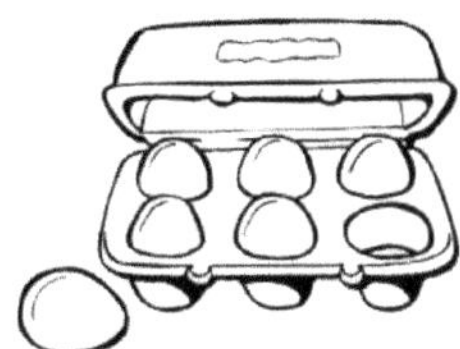

A bakery placed an order for several cartons of 6 eggs. Which of these could be the total number of eggs ordered?

Ⓐ 48

Ⓑ 50

Ⓒ 52

Ⓓ 56

12 The table shows the side length of a square and the area of a square.

Side Length, *x* (inches)	**Area, *y* (square inches)**
2	4
3	9
4	16
5	25

Which equation represents the relationship between side length and area?

Ⓐ $y = x + 2$

Ⓑ $y = 2x$

Ⓒ $y = x \times x$

Ⓓ $y = 4x$

13 The graph below shows the number of different types of trees in an orchard.

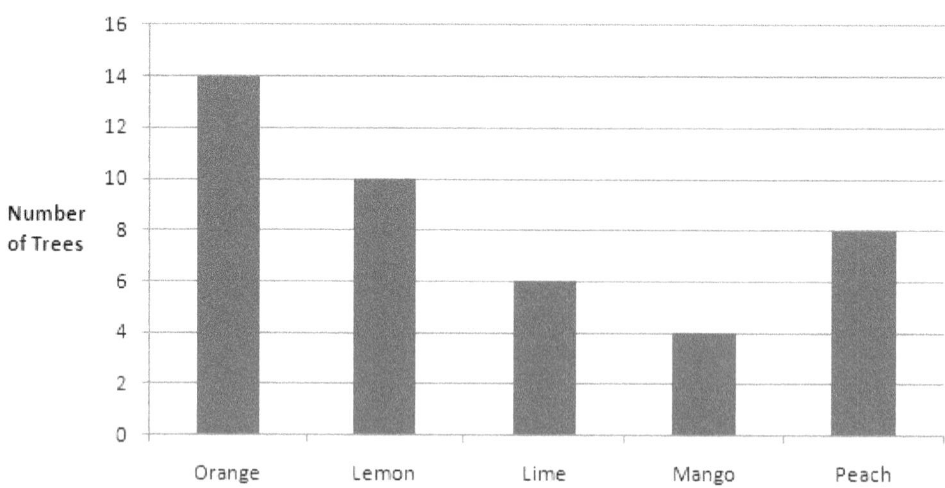

The owner wants to plant more trees so that there are 16 trees of each type. How many more trees does the owner need to plant?

Ⓐ 38

Ⓑ 28

Ⓒ 14

Ⓓ 10

14 Which measurement is the most likely length of a stapler?

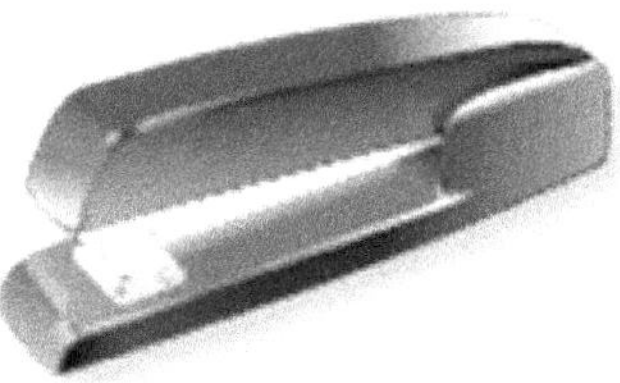

Ⓐ 10 millimetres

Ⓑ 10 centimetres

Ⓒ 10 kilometres

Ⓓ 10 metres

15 Which situation would a circle graph best be used for?

Ⓐ How the number of students at a school has changed over the years

Ⓑ What fraction of people voted for each student in a school election

Ⓒ How the age and height of students is related

Ⓓ What score out of 100 thirty students got on a test

16 Annabelle has 56 1-centimetre cubes. What are the dimensions of a rectangular prism Annabelle could build with all the cubes?

Ⓐ 7 units long, 4 units high, 2 units wide

Ⓑ 6 units long, 5 units high, 5 units wide

Ⓒ 10 units long, 2 units high, 3 units wide

Ⓓ 8 units long, 2 units high, 4 units wide

17 Which number goes in the box to make the equation below true? Write the correct number in the box.

$$\square \div 4 = 7$$

18 Which number is a multiple of 12?

Ⓐ 3

Ⓑ 4

Ⓒ 36

Ⓓ 40

19 Which number comes next in the pattern below?

4, 12, 20, 28, 36, ...

Write your answer on the line below.

____

20 Which statement below is true?

Ⓐ $0.06 < 0.006$

Ⓑ $1.22 < 1.42$

Ⓒ $5.669 < 5.667$

Ⓓ $7.535 < 7.505$

END OF PRACTICE SET

NAPLAN Mathematics

Year 5

Practice Set 3

Instructions

Read each question carefully. For each multiple-choice question, fill in the circle for the correct answer. For other types of questions, follow the directions given in the question.

1 A rectangle has a length of 6 inches and a height of 5 inches. What is the perimeter of the rectangle? Write your answer on the line below.

__________________ inches

2 The diagram below shows two sets of black and white stickers.

Which of the following compares the portion of black stickers in each set?

Ⓐ $\frac{8}{9} > \frac{2}{3}$

Ⓑ $\frac{8}{9} < \frac{2}{9}$

Ⓒ $\frac{2}{3} < \frac{1}{3}$

Ⓓ $\frac{1}{9} > \frac{6}{9}$

3 Which expression represents the fraction of the figure that is shaded?

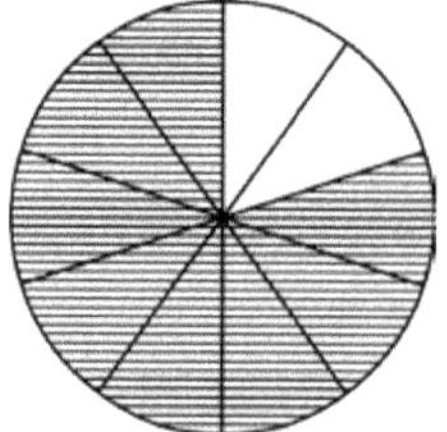

Ⓐ $\frac{1}{10}+\frac{1}{10}+\frac{1}{10}$

Ⓑ $\frac{3}{10}+\frac{3}{10}+\frac{3}{10}$

Ⓒ $\frac{6}{10}+\frac{2}{10}+\frac{2}{10}$

Ⓓ $\frac{3}{10}+\frac{2}{10}+\frac{3}{10}$

4 Maxwell bought a packet of 36 baseball cards. He gave 3 baseball cards to each of 4 friends. Which number sentence can be used to find *c*, the number of baseball cards Maxwell has left?

Ⓐ $36 + (3 + 4) = c$

Ⓑ $36 + (3 \times 4) = c$

Ⓒ $36 - (3 + 4) = c$

Ⓓ $36 - (3 \times 4) = c$

5 A piece of note paper has side lengths of 5 centimetres. What is the perimeter of the note paper?

Ⓐ 10 cm

Ⓑ 20 cm

Ⓒ 25 cm

Ⓓ 30 cm

6 A block is in the shape of a cube. If the side length is represented by s, which of these could be used to find the volume of the cube?

Ⓐ $3s$

Ⓑ $6(s \times s)$

Ⓒ $6s$

Ⓓ $s \times s \times s$

7 Denise made the dot plot below to show how long she read for each weekday for 4 weeks.

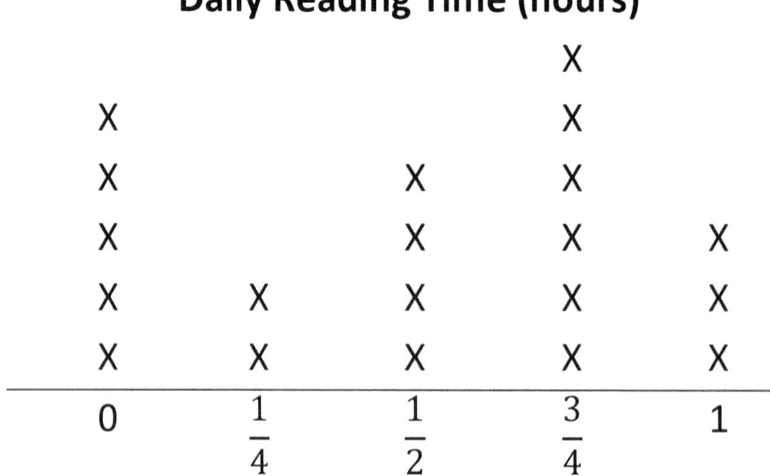

On how many days did Denise read for half an hour or more? Write your answer on the line below.

____

8 Cody drew a quadrilateral on a coordinate grid, as shown below.

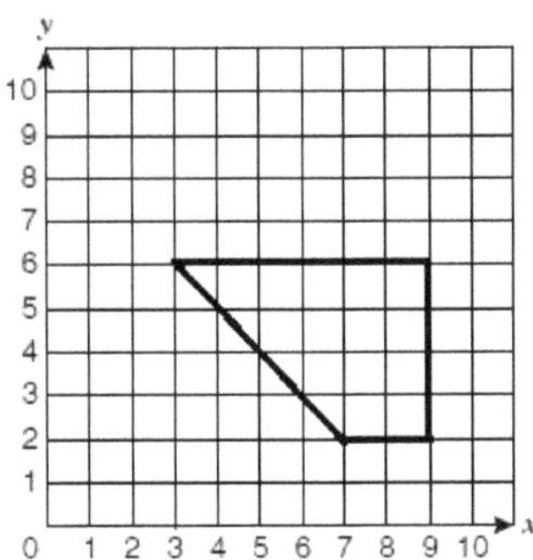

Which of these is **NOT** the coordinates of one of the vertices of the quadrilateral?

Ⓐ (7, 2)

Ⓑ (9, 2)

Ⓒ (6, 9)

Ⓓ (3, 6)

9 If the numbers below were each rounded to the nearest whole number, which number would be rounded down?

Ⓐ 17.386

Ⓑ 35.682

Ⓒ 23.758

Ⓓ 76.935

10 The table below shows the number of male and female students at Hill Street School.

Gender	Number
Male	2,621
Female	2,438

How many more male students are there than female students? Write your answer on the line below.

____

11 A pattern of numbers is shown below.

6, 11, 16, 21, 26, 31, 36, ...

If n is a number in the pattern, which rule can be used to find the next number in the pattern?

Ⓐ $n + 5$

Ⓑ $n - 5$

Ⓒ $n + 6$

Ⓓ $n - 6$

12 A class held a vote on where to go for a field trip. The results are shown below.

Location	**Number of Votes**
Museum	𝍸 𝍸
Cinema	𝍸 |
Zoo	𝍸 𝍸 𝍸 𝍸
Town Hall	||||

Chen decides to make a circle graph to show the results. Which section would make up a quarter of the graph?

Ⓐ Museum

Ⓑ Cinema

Ⓒ Zoo

Ⓓ Town Hall

13 The graph below shows the high temperature in Wollongong for five days.

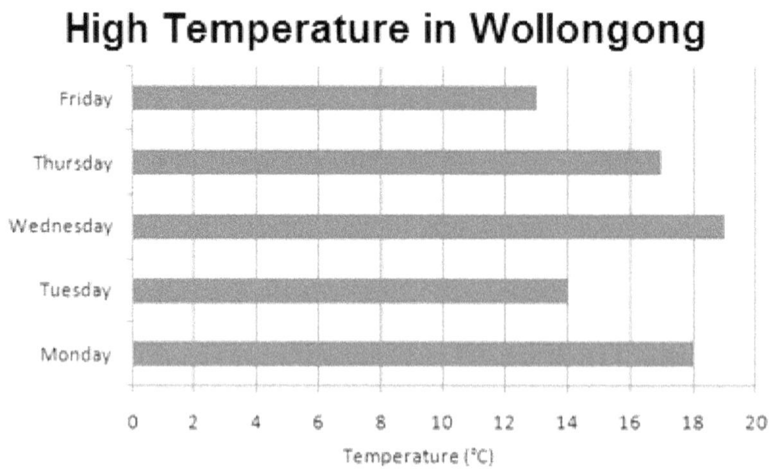

High Temperature in Wollongong

Day	Temperature (°C)
Friday	13
Thursday	17
Wednesday	19
Tuesday	14
Monday	18

On which day was the high temperature 17°C?

Ⓐ Tuesday

Ⓑ Wednesday

Ⓒ Thursday

Ⓓ Friday

14 The graph below shows the line segment *ST*. Point *S* is at (2, 5). Point *T* is at (9, 5).

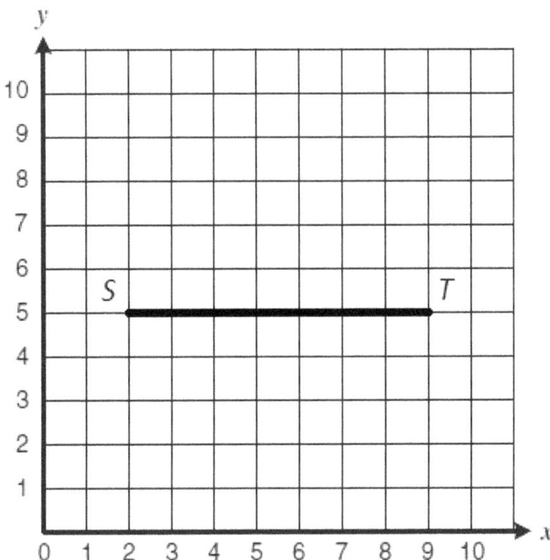

Which of these shows how to find the length of the line segment?

Ⓐ 5 + 5

Ⓑ 9 − 5

Ⓒ 9 − 2

Ⓓ 2 + 9

15 The table below shows the relationship between the original price and the sale price of a book.

Original price, *P*	**Sale price, *S***
\$10	\$5
\$12	\$6
\$14	\$7
\$16	\$8

What is the rule to find the sale price of a book, in dollars?

Ⓐ $S = P \div 2$

Ⓑ $S = P \times 2$

Ⓒ $S = P - 2$

Ⓓ $S = P + 2$

16 A standard coin is tossed. What is the probability that the coin lands on either heads or tails?

Ⓐ 0

Ⓑ 0.25

Ⓒ 0.5

Ⓓ 1

17 Which decimal is represented below?

$$(6 \times 10) + (3 \times 1) + (9 \times \frac{1}{10}) + (4 \times \frac{1}{1000})$$

Ⓐ 63.094

Ⓑ 63.904

Ⓒ 63.94

Ⓓ 63.9004

18 Jonah filled the box below with 1-inch cubes. How many 1-inch cubes would it take to fill the box?

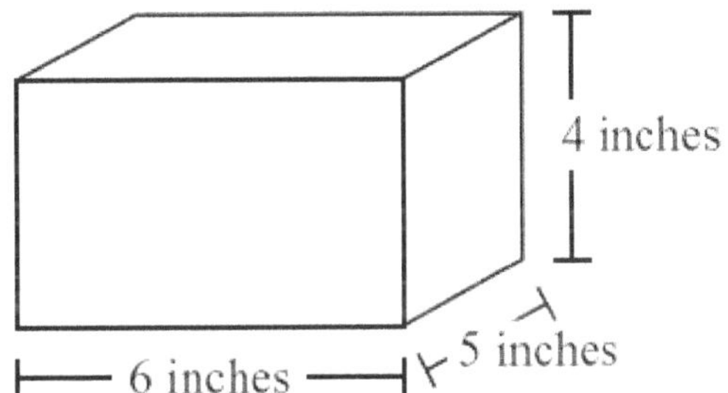

Write your answer on the line below.

____

19 The dot plot below shows the number of athletics events entered by each student in a class.

Number of Athletics Events Entered

		X		
		X	X	
X		X	X	
X	X	X	X	
X	X	X	X	X
X	X	X	X	X
1	2	3	4	5

What fraction of the students entered 5 events?

Ⓐ $\frac{1}{5}$

Ⓑ $\frac{1}{2}$

Ⓒ $\frac{1}{9}$

Ⓓ $\frac{1}{10}$

20 Mr. Daniels has a business meeting at 7:15 p.m. Which of these gives the time of the business meeting in 24-hour time?

Ⓐ 7:15

Ⓑ 17:15

Ⓒ 19:15

Ⓓ 21:15

END OF PRACTICE SET

NAPLAN Mathematics

Year 5

Practice Test 1

Instructions

Read each question carefully. For each multiple-choice question, fill in the circle for the correct answer. For other types of questions, follow the directions given in the question.

1 Troy recorded the number of sales he made each month.

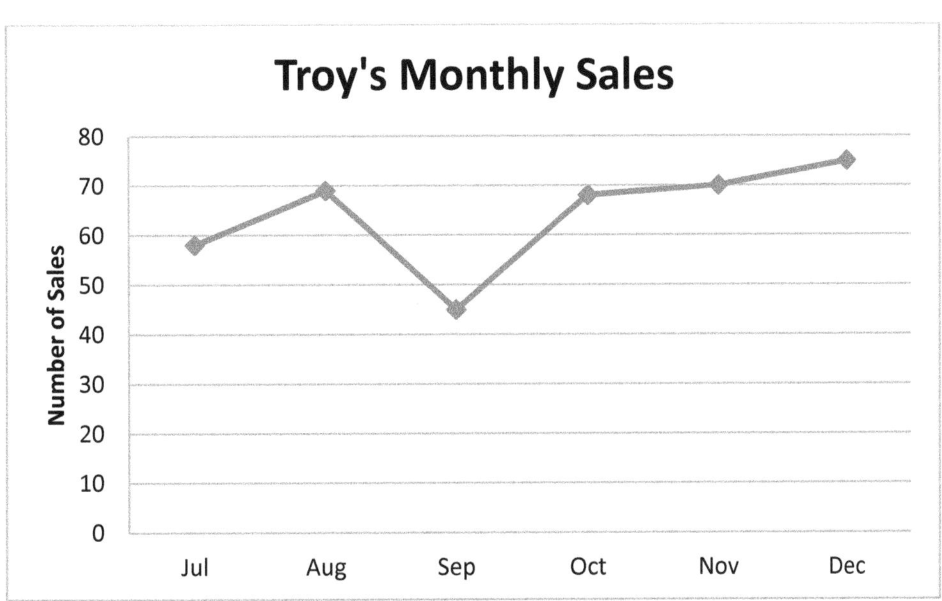

Between which two months did Troy's sales increase the most?

Ⓐ July to August

Ⓑ August to September

Ⓒ September to October

Ⓓ November to December

2 A school has 7 school buses. Each bus can seat 48 students. A total of 303 students get on the buses to go to a school camp. How many empty seats would there be on the buses? Write your answer on the line below.

____

3 A fraction representing $\frac{6}{8}$ is shown below.

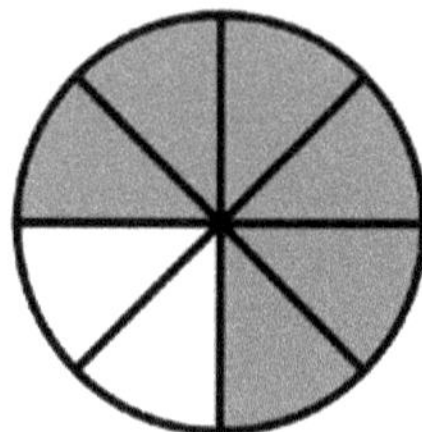

Which of these is the same as $\frac{6}{8}$?

Ⓐ $\frac{1}{2}+\frac{1}{2}+\frac{1}{2}$

Ⓑ $\frac{1}{4}+\frac{1}{4}+\frac{1}{4}$

Ⓒ $\frac{1}{6}+\frac{1}{6}+\frac{1}{6}$

Ⓓ $\frac{1}{8}+\frac{1}{8}+\frac{1}{8}$

4 The table below shows the number of students in each year at the David Hall School.

Year	Number of Students
3	254
4	235
5	229

How many students are there all together? Write your answer on the line below.

____

5 A square garden has side lengths of 8 feet. What is the area of the garden? You can use the diagram below to help find the answer.

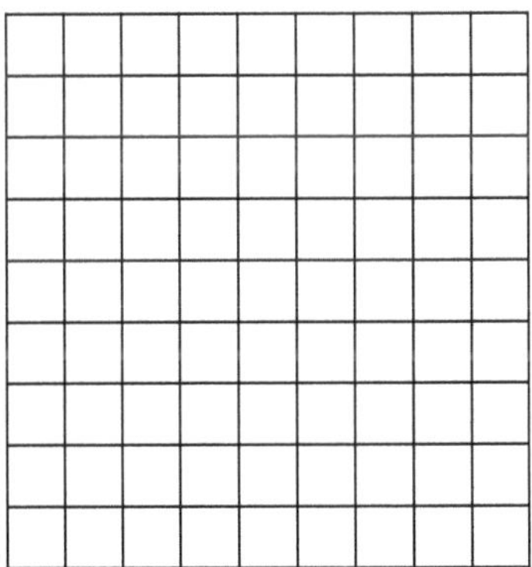

Write your answer on the line below.

____________________ square feet

6 A box contains 24 cans of soups. Gerald orders 8 boxes of soup for his store. He is charged $0.50 for each can of soup. What is the total cost of the soup Gerald ordered?

Ⓐ $12

Ⓑ $64

Ⓒ $96

Ⓓ $384

7 Which ordered pair represents a point located inside both rectangles?

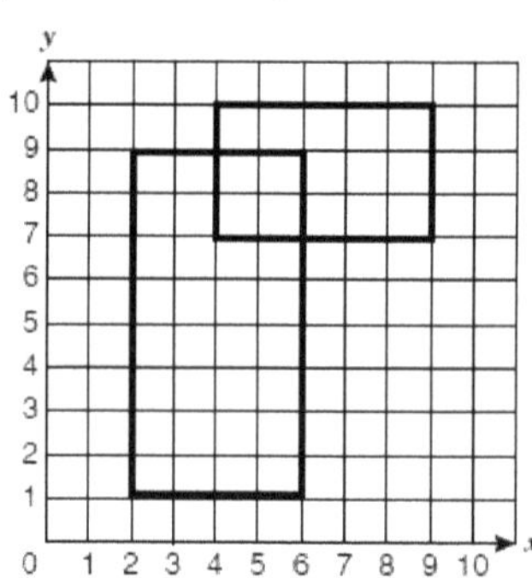

Ⓐ (8, 6)

Ⓑ (5, 8)

Ⓒ (4, 10)

Ⓓ (7, 9)

8 How is the numeral 35.012 written in words?

Ⓐ Thirty-five thousand and twelve

Ⓑ Thirty-five and twelve thousandths

Ⓒ Thirty-five and twelve hundredths

Ⓓ Thirty-five and twelve

9 Which point represents the location of the ordered pair $(1\frac{1}{4}, 2\frac{1}{2})$?

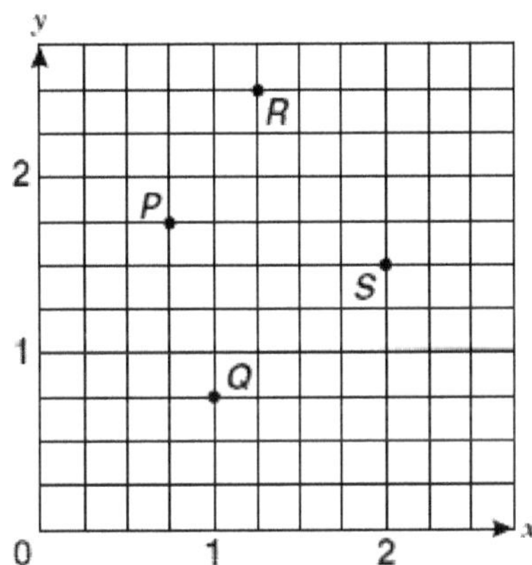

Ⓐ Point *P*

Ⓑ Point *Q*

Ⓒ Point *R*

Ⓓ Point *S*

10 The 5 letter cards below are placed on a table. Baxter picks a letter card at random.

T

S

What is the probability that Baxter will pick a vowel?

Ⓐ 2 out of 3

Ⓑ 2 out of 5

Ⓒ 1 out of 2

Ⓓ 3 out of 5

11 What is the most likely mass of the bicycle shown below?

Ⓐ 1 g

Ⓑ 100 g

Ⓒ 10 kg

Ⓓ 1000 kg

12 Victor rode 3.65 kilometres to his friend's house. How many metres did Victor ride?

Ⓐ 365 metres

Ⓑ 3,650 metres

Ⓒ 36,500 metres

Ⓓ 365,000 metres

13 The table below shows the temperature recorded each hour from 9 a.m. to 2 p.m.

Time	Temperature (°C)
9 a.m.	8
10 a.m.	11
11 a.m.	13
12 noon	16
1 p.m.	17
2 p.m.	19

Steve wants to draw a graph to show how the temperature changed from 9 a.m. to 2 p.m. Which type of graph would Steve be best to use?

Ⓐ Circle graph

Ⓑ Line graph

Ⓒ Picture graph

Ⓓ Dot plot

14 The fine for having a DVD overdue is a basic fee of \$4 plus an additional \$2 for each day that the movie is overdue. Which equation can be used to find c, the cost in dollars of the fine for d days?

Ⓐ $c = 2d + 4$

Ⓑ $c = 4d + 2$

Ⓒ $c = 2(d + 4)$

Ⓓ $c = 4(d + 2)$

15 Leonard bought 12 tickets to a charity event. The total cost of the tickets was \$216. The expression below can be used to find the cost of each ticket.

$$216 \div 12$$

Which of the following is equivalent to the above expression?

Ⓐ $(240 \div 12) + (24 \div 12)$

Ⓑ $(200 \div 10) + (16 \div 2)$

Ⓒ $(216 \div 10) + (216 \div 2)$

Ⓓ $(120 \div 12) + (96 \div 12)$

16 What is the perimeter of the rectangle shown below?

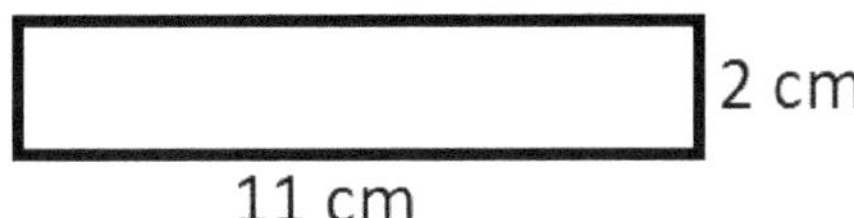

Write your answer on the line below.

____________________ cm

17 Which figure has $\frac{1}{4}$ shaded?

Ⓐ 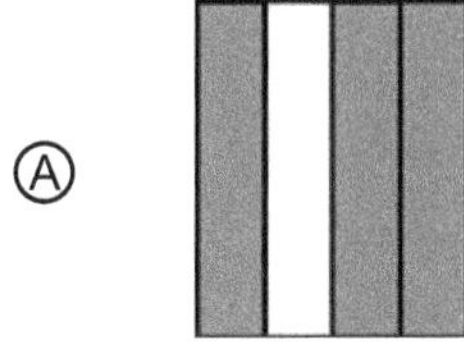

Ⓑ 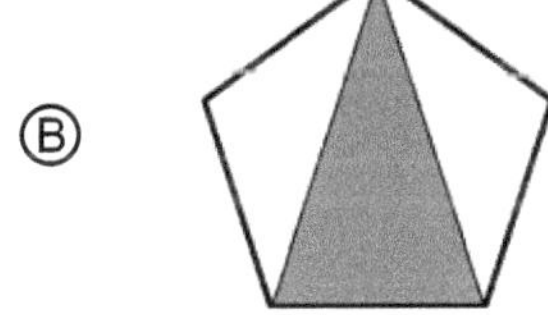

Ⓒ 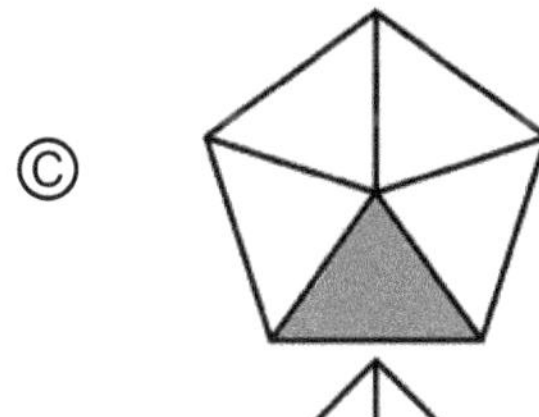

Ⓓ 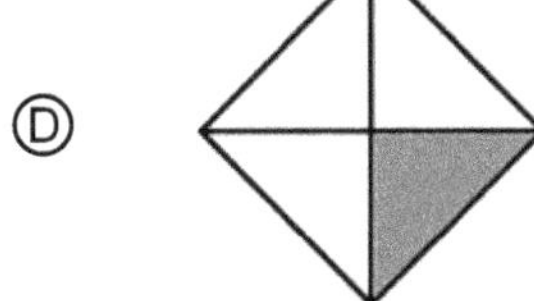

18 Winona has 48 stamps. She has 6 times as many stamps as Catherine. How many stamps does Catherine have? Write your answer on the line below.

____

19 What is the value of $1\frac{2}{5} \div 2$? You can use the model below to help find the answer.

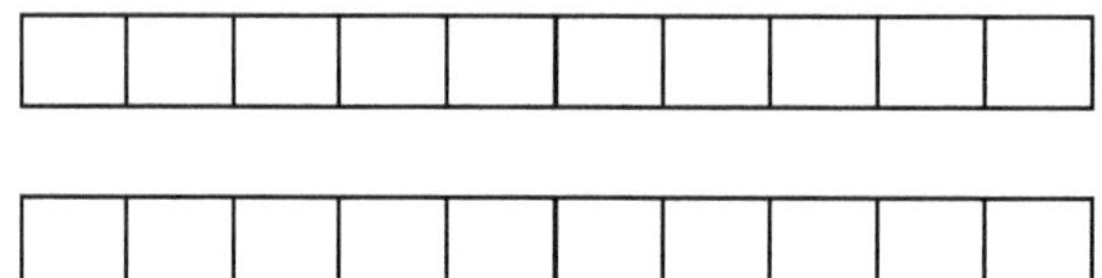

Ⓐ $\frac{1}{6}$

Ⓑ $\frac{2}{7}$

Ⓒ $\frac{7}{10}$

Ⓓ $1\frac{1}{5}$

20 The factor tree for the number 60 is shown below.

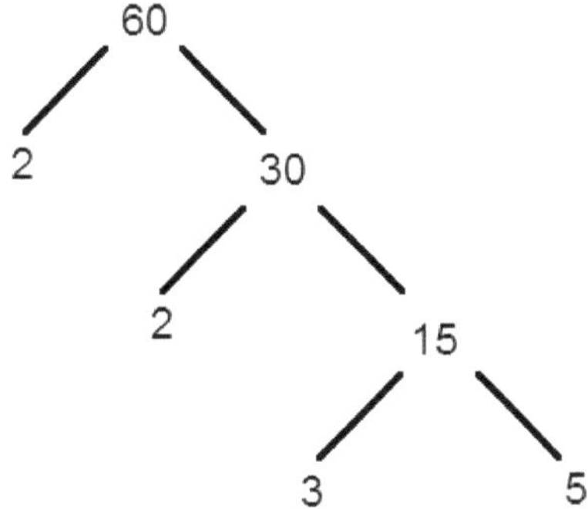

According to the factor tree, which statement is true?

Ⓐ The number 30 is prime.

Ⓑ The only prime factor of 60 is 2.

Ⓒ The numbers 15 and 30 are prime factors of 60.

Ⓓ The numbers 2, 3, and 5 are prime factors of 60.

21 The table below shows the total number of kilograms of flour in different numbers of bags of flour.

Number of Bags	Number of Kilograms
3	12
5	20
8	32
9	36

What is the relationship between the number of bags of flour and the number of kilograms of flour?

Ⓐ The number of kilograms is 9 more than the number of bags.

Ⓑ The number of kilograms is 15 more than the number of bags.

Ⓒ The number of kilograms is 4 times the number of bags.

Ⓓ The number of kilograms is 6 times the number of bags.

22 Which is the best way to estimate the product of 28 and 44?

Ⓐ 20×40

Ⓑ 20×50

Ⓒ 30×40

Ⓓ 30×50

23 The model below is made up of 1-centimeter cubes.

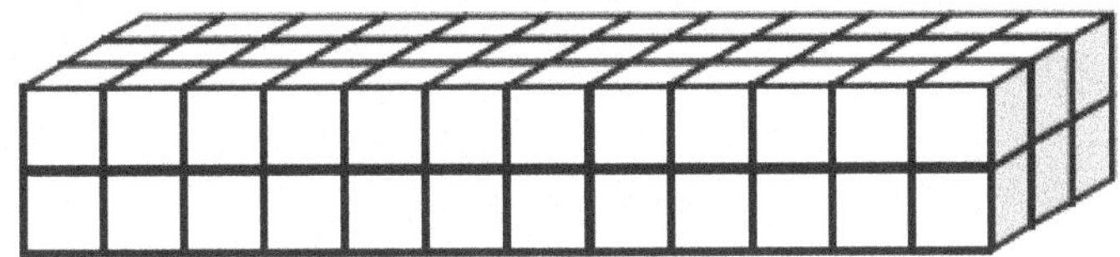

What is a correct way to find the volume of the model?

Ⓐ 12 cm x 6 cm

Ⓑ 2 cm x 6 cm x 12 cm

Ⓒ 2 cm x 3 cm x 12 cm

Ⓓ 12 cm x 12 cm

24 How many centimetres are equivalent to 400 millimetres?

Ⓐ 0.4 cm

Ⓑ 4 cm

Ⓒ 40 cm

Ⓓ 4000 cm

25 Jordan's flight to Perth leaves at 2:20 in the afternoon. Which of these gives the time the flight leaves in 24-hour time?

Ⓐ 10:20

Ⓑ 12:20

Ⓒ 14:20

Ⓓ 20:20

26 A square poster has side lengths of 8 inches. What is the area of the poster?

Ⓐ 32 square inches

Ⓑ 36 square inches

Ⓒ 48 square inches

Ⓓ 64 square inches

27 Tom worked for 32 hours and earned $448. He earned the same rate per hour. How much does Tom earn per hour? Write your answer on the line below.

$ ______________________

28 Joe made the graph below to show the locations of prizes he hid for a treasure hunt. Each star represents a treasure.

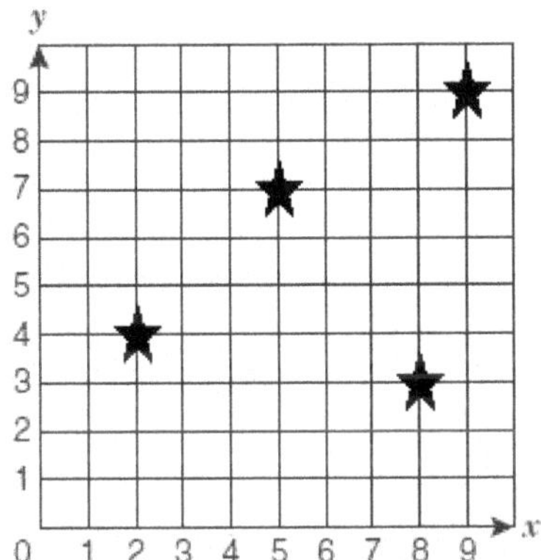

Samantha started searching at the origin. Which ordered pair represents the location of the treasure closest to Samantha?

Ⓐ (2, 4)

Ⓑ (5, 7)

Ⓒ (8, 3)

Ⓓ (9, 9)

29 Which single transformation is represented in the models of the lightning bolts?

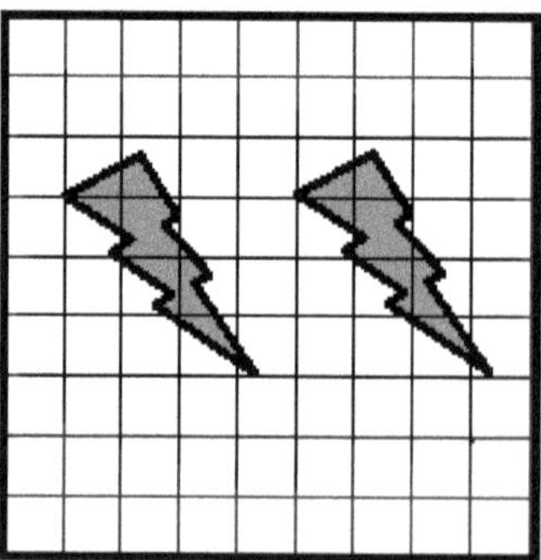

Ⓐ Reflection

Ⓑ Translation

Ⓒ Rotation

Ⓓ Dilation

30 William surveyed students on how long it took them to travel to school each morning. The table shows the results.

Time	Number of Students
0 to 10 minutes	22
11 to 30 minutes	36
31 to 60 minutes	14
Over 60 minutes	3

Daniella travels to school in a time that is in the most common time range. Which of the following could be the time it takes Daniella to travel to school?

Ⓐ 18 minutes

Ⓑ 65 minutes

Ⓒ 7 minutes

Ⓓ 33 minutes

31 To complete a calculation correctly, Mark moves the decimal place of 420.598 two places to the left.

$$420.598 \rightarrow 4.20598$$

Which of these describes the calculation completed?

Ⓐ Dividing by 10

Ⓑ Dividing by 100

Ⓒ Multiplying by 10

Ⓓ Multiplying by 100

32 If the numbers below were each rounded to the nearest tenth, which number would be rounded down?

Ⓐ 17.386

Ⓑ 23.758

Ⓒ 35.672

Ⓓ 54.127

33 The graph below shows data a science class collected on the diameter of pebbles collected on a beach.

Pebble Diameter (inches)

		X						
		X		X	X			
		X	X	X	X	X	X	
0	$\frac{1}{8}$	$\frac{1}{4}$	$\frac{3}{8}$	$\frac{1}{2}$	$\frac{5}{8}$	$\frac{3}{4}$	$\frac{7}{8}$	1

How many pebbles had diameters of $\frac{1}{2}$ inch or more? Write your answer on the line below.

____

34 What is the measure of the angle shown below?

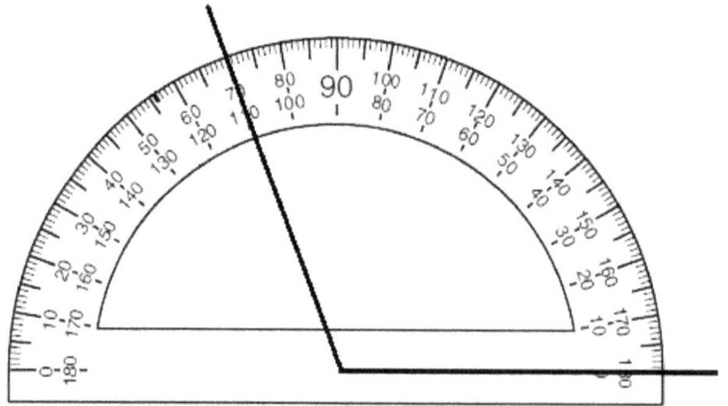

Ⓐ 20°

Ⓑ 70°

Ⓒ 110°

Ⓓ 120°

35 The table below shows the total cost of hiring DVDs for different numbers of DVDs.

Number of DVDs	Total Cost
2	$6
5	$15
6	$18
8	$24

Which equation could be used to find the total cost, c, of hiring x DVDs?

Ⓐ $c = x + 4$

Ⓑ $c = 3x$

Ⓒ $c = x + 3$

Ⓓ $c = 8x$

36 Dave bought 4 packets of pies. Three packets had 12 pies each, and one packet had 10 pies. Which number sentence shows the total number of pies Dave bought?

Ⓐ (3 x 12) x 10

Ⓑ (3 + 12) x 10

Ⓒ (3 x 12) + 10

Ⓓ (3 + 12) + 10

37 The dot plot below shows how many goals each member of a soccer team scored in the season.

Soccer Goals

X	X			
X	X	X		
X	X	X	X	
X	X	X	X	X
0	1	2	3	4

Which statement is true?

Ⓐ Each player scored at least 1 goal.

Ⓑ Only one player scored more than 3 goals.

Ⓒ The same number of players scored 2 goals as scored 3 goals.

Ⓓ More players scored 1 goal than scored no goals.

38 The grid below represents Dani's living room.

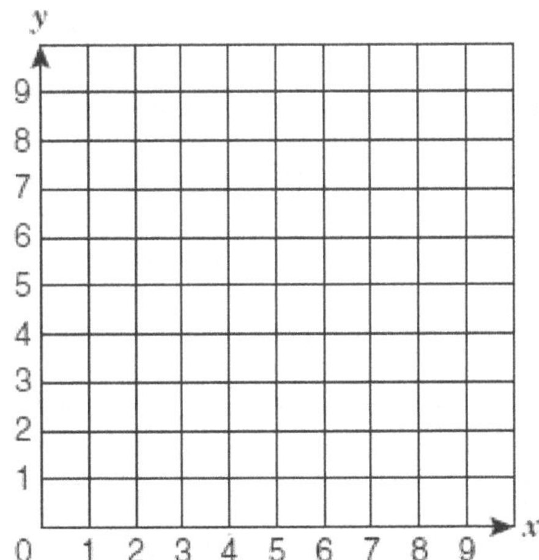

The television is located at the point (5, 4). A lamp is sitting 4 units to the right of the television and 3 units down from the television. Which ordered pair represents the location of the lamp?

Ⓐ (0, 2)

Ⓑ (1, 1)

Ⓒ (8, 2)

Ⓓ (9, 1)

39 The table below shows the number of households in four different suburbs.

Suburb	Number of Households
Wellington	135,682
Ashton	179,441
Ellis	120,597
Mayfield	191,822

How many more households does Mayfield have than Ashton? Write your answer on the line below.

____

40 A rectangular toy box has a length of 90 centimetres, a width of 30 centimetres, and a height of 50 centimetres. What is the volume of the toy box?

Ⓐ 4,500 cubic centimetres

Ⓑ 6,000 cubic centimetres

Ⓒ 81,000 cubic centimetres

Ⓓ 135,000 cubic centimetres

END OF PRACTICE TEST

NAPLAN Mathematics

Year 5

Practice Test 2

Instructions

Read each question carefully. For each multiple-choice question, fill in the circle for the correct answer. For other types of questions, follow the directions given in the question.

1 Which number is the greatest?

Ⓐ 65.029

Ⓑ 65.061

Ⓒ 65.101

Ⓓ 65.125

2 Trevor's baby sister had a nap for $1\frac{3}{4}$ hours. How many minutes did she nap for? Write your answer on the line below.

_______________ minutes

3 Which pair of figures shows a reflection?

Ⓐ 

Ⓑ 

Ⓒ 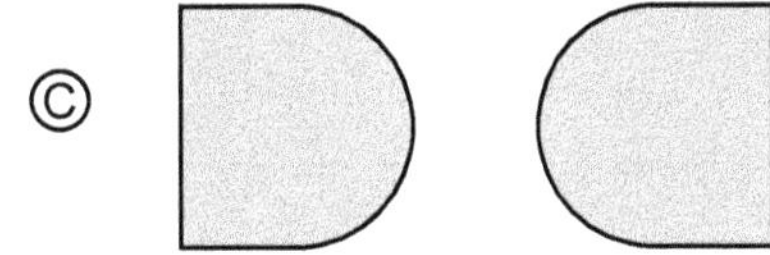

Ⓓ 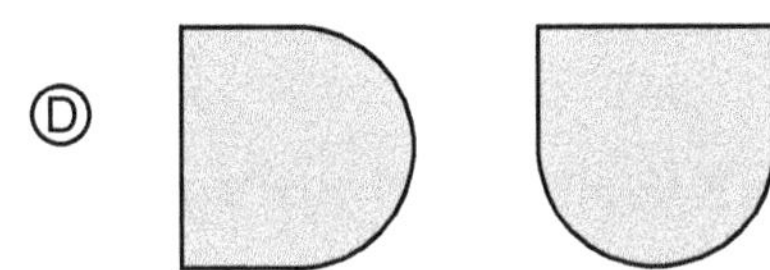

4 Which number is a multiple of 8?

Ⓐ 42

Ⓑ 44

Ⓒ 52

Ⓓ 56

5 A fish tank can hold 20 litres of water. How many millilitres of water can the fish tank hold?

Ⓐ 200 millilitres

Ⓑ 2,000 millilitres

Ⓒ 20,000 millilitres

Ⓓ 200,000 millilitres

6 A pattern of numbers is shown below.

8, 13, 18, 23, 28, 33, 38, ...

What is the next number in the pattern? Write your answer on the line below.

____

7 Glenn has 7 ties in his drawer. There are 5 plain ties and 2 patterned ties. If Glenn selects one tie without looking, what is the probability that he will select a plain tie?

Ⓐ 2 out of 7

Ⓑ 2 out of 5

Ⓒ 5 out of 7

Ⓓ 7 out of 10

8 Bryant was reading a book with 220 pages. He read 90 pages in the first week. He wants to finish the book in 5 days. Which expression can be used to calculate how many pages he needs to read each day to finish the book in 5 days?

Ⓐ $220 \div 5 - 90$

Ⓑ $220 - 90 \div 5$

Ⓒ $220 - (90 \div 5)$

Ⓓ $(220 - 90) \div 5$

9 Which of these units would be best to use to measure the mass of a laptop computer?

Ⓐ Milligrams

Ⓑ Kilograms

Ⓒ Centimetres

Ⓓ Metres

10 The table below shows a set of number pairs.

x	y
1	1
3	5
5	9

Which equation shows the relationship between x and y?

Ⓐ $y = x + 2$

Ⓑ $y = x + 4$

Ⓒ $y = 2x - 1$

Ⓓ $y = 3x - 4$

11 Which transformation is shown below?

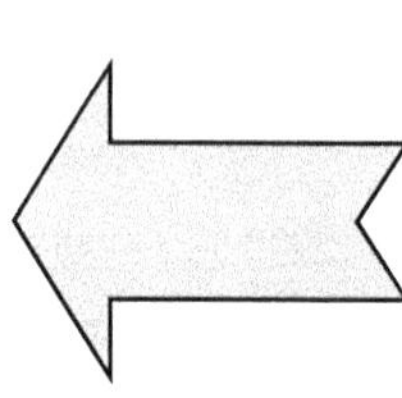

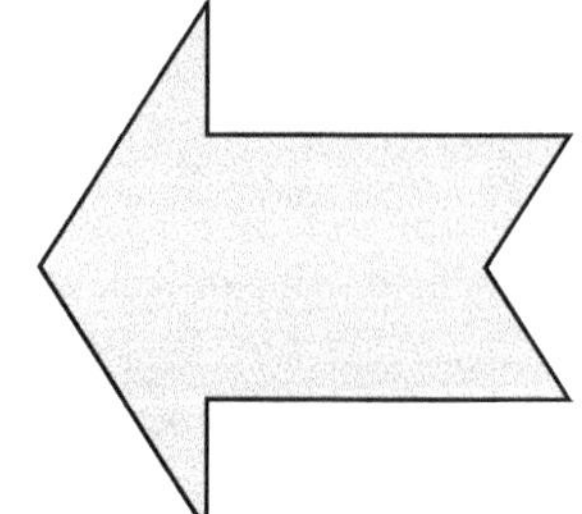

Ⓐ Rotation

Ⓑ Reflection

Ⓒ Translation

Ⓓ Dilation

12 The graph below shows data a science class collected on the diameter of hailstones that fell during a storm.

Hailstone Diameter (inches)

		X						
		X		X	X			
		X	X	X	X	X	X	
0	$\frac{1}{8}$	$\frac{1}{4}$	$\frac{3}{8}$	$\frac{1}{2}$	$\frac{5}{8}$	$\frac{3}{4}$	$\frac{7}{8}$	1

How many hailstones had diameters of $\frac{1}{2}$ inch or more? Write your answer on the line below.

____

13 Joy made an apple pie. Joy and her 3 children ate $\frac{5}{8}$ of the apple pie.

What fraction of the apple pie would be left over?

Ⓐ $\frac{9}{8}$

Ⓑ $\frac{3}{8}$

Ⓒ $\frac{5}{12}$

Ⓓ $\frac{5}{32}$

14 The graph below shows the line segment *PQ*. Point *P* is at (3, 9). Point *Q* is at (3, 1).

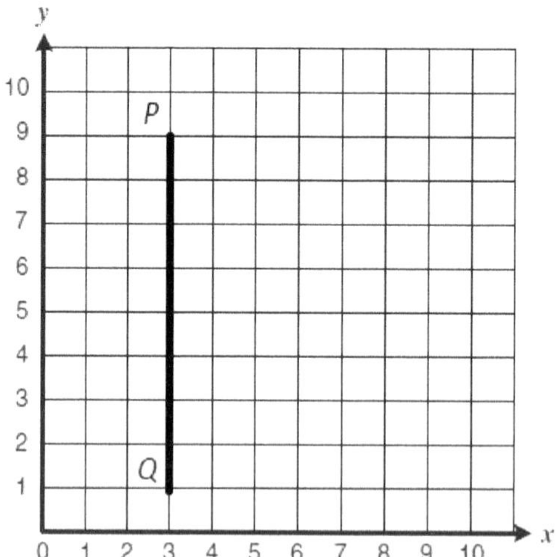

What is the length of the line segment *PQ*?

Ⓐ 3 units

Ⓑ 8 units

Ⓒ 9 units

Ⓓ 10 units

15 The factor tree for the number 36 is shown below.

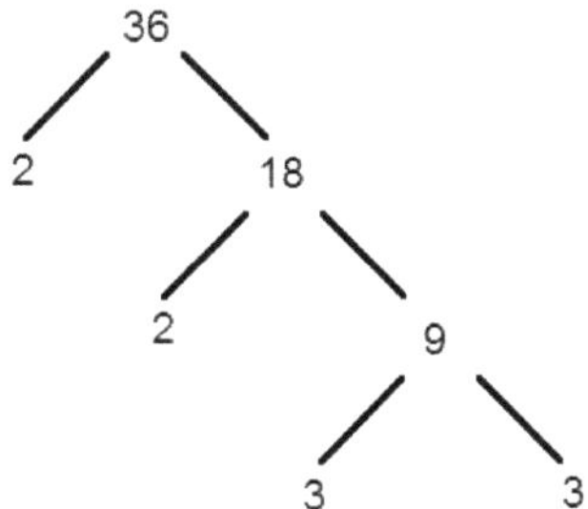

Which number is a prime factor of 36?

Ⓐ 3

Ⓑ 6

Ⓒ 9

Ⓓ 18

16 An orchard has a total of 1,176 orange trees. They are planted in rows of 12 orange trees each. How many rows of orange trees does the orchard have? Write your answer on the line below.

____

17 Which number makes the number sentence below true? Write the correct number in the box.

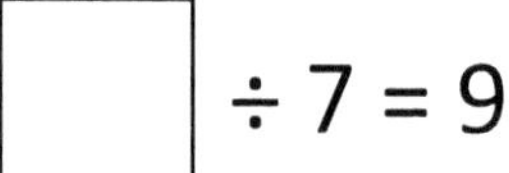

18 Which number is a factor of the number 40?

Ⓐ 3

Ⓑ 6

Ⓒ 7

Ⓓ 8

19 Leanne added $\frac{1}{4}$ cup of milk and $\frac{3}{8}$ cup of water to a bowl. Which diagram is shaded to show how many cups of milk and water were in the bowl in all?

Ⓐ 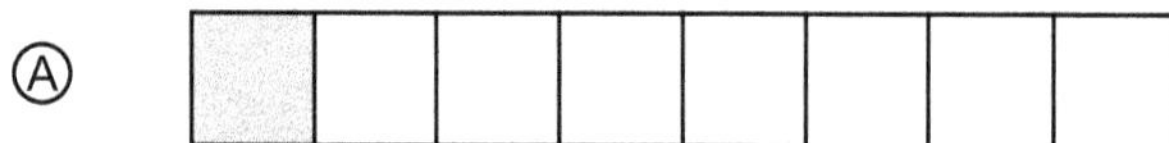

Ⓑ 

Ⓒ 

Ⓓ

20 Which decimal is represented below?

$$(4 \times 100) + (8 \times 1) + (6 \times \frac{1}{100}) + (3 \times \frac{1}{1000})$$

Ⓐ 480.63

Ⓑ 480.063

Ⓒ 408.63

Ⓓ 408.063

21 Tomato plants were planted in rows. Each row had the same number of tomato plants.

Number of Rows	Number of Tomato Plants
3	24
4	32
5	40
6	48

Based on the table above, how many tomato plants were in each row? Write your answer on the line below.

____

22 The graph below shows a line segment with 3 points marked.

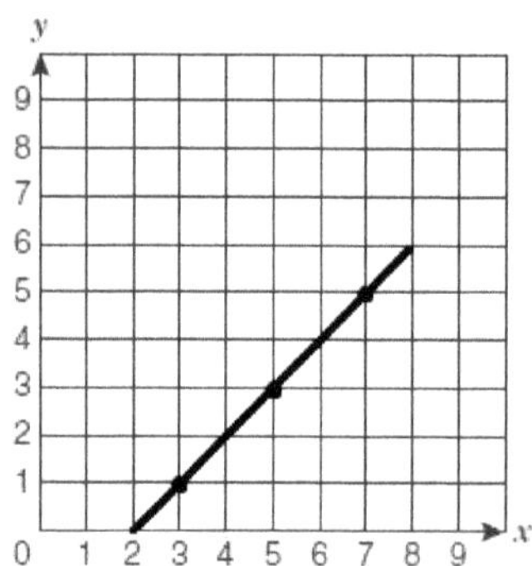

Which table shows the coordinates of these 3 points?

Ⓐ

x	1	2	3
y	3	5	7

Ⓑ

x	3	5	7
y	1	3	5

Ⓒ

x	1	3	5
y	1	2	3

Ⓓ

x	1	3	5
y	3	5	7

23 Brian made 16 paper cranes in 15 minutes. If he continues making cranes at this rate, how many cranes would he make in 2 hours?

Ⓐ 32

Ⓑ 64

Ⓒ 120

Ⓓ 128

24 The cost of renting a windsurfer is a basic fee of $15 plus an additional $5 for each hour that the windsurfer is rented. Which equation can be used to find *c*, the cost in dollars of the rental for *h* hours?

Ⓐ $c = 15h + 5$

Ⓑ $c = 5h + 15$

Ⓒ $c = 15(h + 5)$

Ⓓ $c = 5(h + 15)$

25 Amanda plotted the four points below on a coordinate grid.

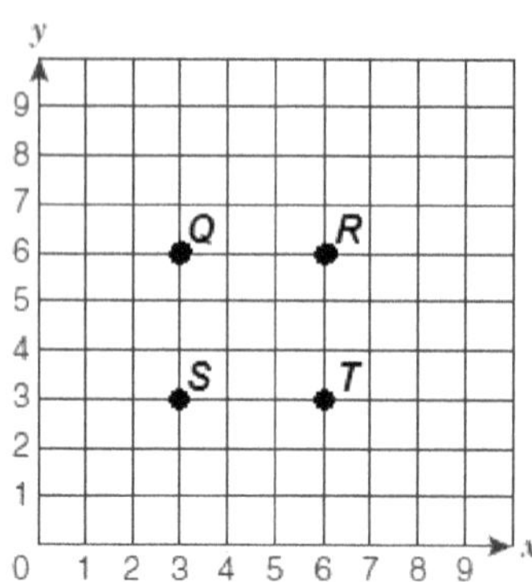

Amanda plots a fifth point that is an equal distance from two of the points. Which of these could be the coordinates of the fifth point?

Ⓐ (5, 8)

Ⓑ (3.5, 5)

Ⓒ (7, 7)

Ⓓ (9, 4.5)

26 Joy made 24 apple pies for a bake sale. Each serving was $\frac{1}{8}$ of a pie.

How many servings did Joy make?

Ⓐ 3

Ⓑ 32

Ⓒ 96

Ⓓ 192

27 The model below is made up of 1-centimeter cubes. What is a correct way to find the volume of the cube, in cubic centimetres?

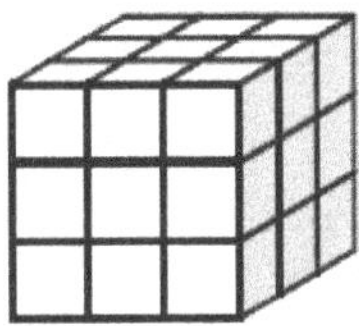

Ⓐ 3 + 3 + 3

Ⓑ 3 × 3 × 3

Ⓒ 3 × 3

Ⓓ 6(3 × 3)

28 What is the decimal 55.146 rounded to the nearest tenth? Write your answer on the line below.

____

29 Which ordered pair represents a point located on the line?

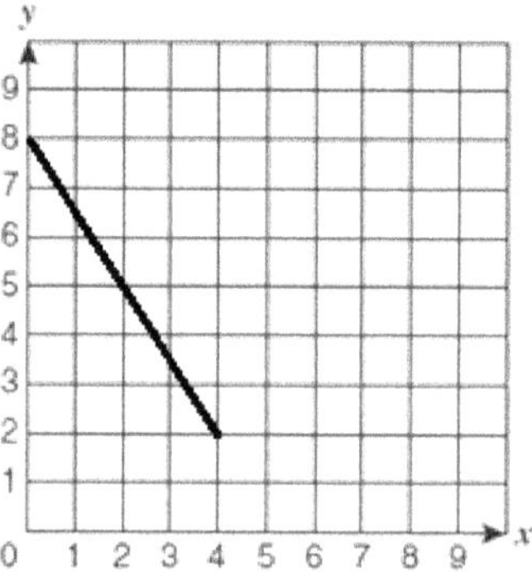

Ⓐ (8, 0)

Ⓑ (4, 2)

Ⓒ (3, 3)

Ⓓ (5, 2)

30 Kyla's class is going to raise money for a class trip by holding a talent contest. It will cost $200 to organise the talent contest. The class wants to make $500 profit. How many tickets of $10 each will need to be sold to make $500 profit?

Ⓐ 20

Ⓑ 30

Ⓒ 50

Ⓓ 70

31 What is the measure of the angle shown below?

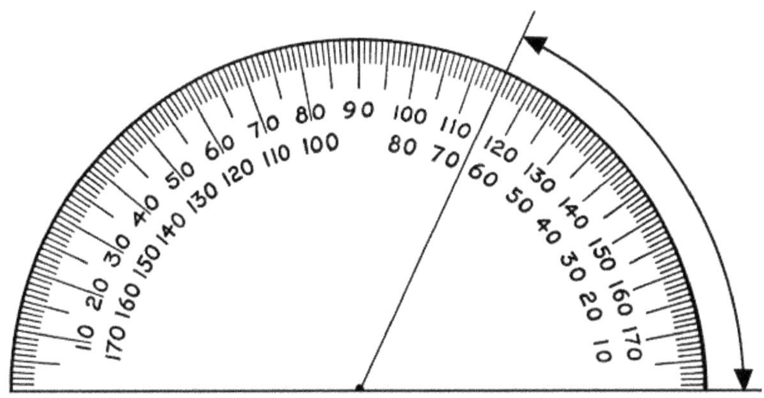

Ⓐ 65°

Ⓑ 75°

Ⓒ 115°

Ⓓ 125°

32 The table below shows the total number of lemons in different numbers of bags of lemons.

Number of Bags	Number of Lemons
2	16
3	24
5	40
8	64

What is the relationship between the number of bags of lemons and the total number of lemons?

Ⓐ The number of lemons is 8 more than the number of bags.

Ⓑ The number of lemons is 16 more than the number of bags.

Ⓒ The number of lemons is 8 times the number of bags.

Ⓓ The number of lemons is 16 times the number of bags.

33 Amy ordered 3 pizzas for $6.95 each. She also bought a soft drink for $1.95. Which equation can be used to find how much change, *c*, she should receive from $30?

Ⓐ $c = 30 - 3(6.95 + 1.95)$

Ⓑ $c = 30 - 3(6.95 - 1.95)$

Ⓒ $c = 30 - 6.95 - 1.95$

Ⓓ $c = 30 - (6.95 \times 3) - 1.95$

34 How is the numeral 55.12 written in words?

Ⓐ Fifty-five hundred and twelve

Ⓑ Fifty-five and twelve thousandths

Ⓒ Fifty-five and twelve hundredths

Ⓓ Fifty-five and twelve

35 Which number is greater than 0.75?

Ⓐ 0.68

Ⓑ 0.72

Ⓒ 0.79

Ⓓ 0.57

36 Wyatt made the grid below to show the locations of his home, w, and the locations of his friends.

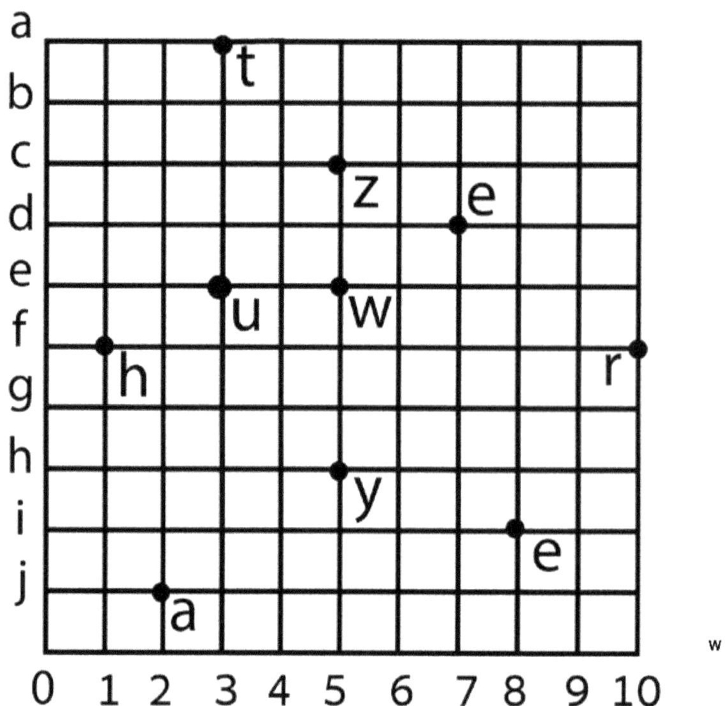

Which friend could Wyatt visit by travelling directly south without making any turns?

Ⓐ Zoe, represented by z

Ⓑ Hank, represented by h

Ⓒ Ursula, represented by u

Ⓓ Yvonne, represented by y

37 The table shows the side length of a rhombus and the perimeter of a rhombus.

Side Length, x (cm)	Perimeter, y (cm)
1	4
2	8
3	12
4	16

Which equation represents the relationship between side length and perimeter?

Ⓐ $y = x + 3$

Ⓑ $y = 4x$

Ⓒ $x = y + 4$

Ⓓ $x = 4y$

38 What is the value of $\frac{9}{12} - \frac{3}{12}$?

Ⓐ $\frac{1}{12}$

Ⓑ $\frac{3}{12}$

Ⓒ $\frac{5}{12}$

Ⓓ $\frac{6}{12}$

39 What is the area of the square below?

6 cm

Ⓐ $12\ cm^2$

Ⓑ $24\ cm^2$

Ⓒ $30\ cm^2$

Ⓓ $36\ cm^2$

40 It took James and his family $2\frac{1}{4}$ hours to drive from their house to the beach. How many minutes did the drive take? Write your answer on the line below.

__________________ minutes

END OF PRACTICE TEST

NAPLAN Mathematics

Year 5

Practice Test 3

Instructions

Read each question carefully. For each multiple-choice question, fill in the circle for the correct answer. For other types of questions, follow the directions given in the question.

1 A pattern has the rule $y = 4x - 1$. What is the value of y when $x = 6$?

Ⓐ 9

Ⓑ 18

Ⓒ 20

Ⓓ 23

2 Sam has 15 DVDs in her bookcase. The table below shows the different types of DVDs Sam has in her bookcase.

Type of DVD	Number of DVDs
Action	3
Comedy	7
Drama	4
Science fiction	1

If Sam picks 1 DVD from the bookcase without looking, what is the probability that she will pick a comedy?

Ⓐ $\frac{7}{15}$

Ⓑ $\frac{4}{15}$

Ⓒ $\frac{3}{12}$

Ⓓ $\frac{7}{8}$

3 Dora bought 4 packets of pens. She bought 36 pens in all. Which equation can be used to find how many pens, *p*, were in each packet?

Ⓐ $p \div 36 = 4$

Ⓑ $36 \div p = 4$

Ⓒ $36 \times 4 = p$

Ⓓ $36 \times p = 4$

4 The top of a desk is 4 metres long and 3 metres wide. Raymond wants to find the area of the desk. What is the area of the top of the desk? Write your answer on the line below.

____________________ square metres

5 The cost of renting a trailer is a basic fee of $20 plus an additional $25 for each day that the trailer is rented. The cost, c, is represented by the equation below, where d is the number of days.

$$c = 25d + 20$$

How much would it cost to rent a trailer for 5 days?

Ⓐ $50

Ⓑ $145

Ⓒ $225

Ⓓ $625

6 Brett surveys students and asks them how long they studied for a test. He wants to make a chart to see if there is a relationship between the time studied and the test score. What type of chart would Brett be best to use?

Ⓐ Dot plot

Ⓑ Picture graph

Ⓒ Scatterplot

Ⓓ Bar graph

7 Which statement is true?

Ⓐ $48.06 < 47.65$

Ⓑ $32.55 < 32.09$

Ⓒ $27.09 < 27.16$

Ⓓ $11.88 < 11.73$

8 What is the value of $\frac{3}{10} + \frac{6}{10}$?

Ⓐ $\frac{9}{10}$

Ⓑ $\frac{9}{20}$

Ⓒ $\frac{9}{100}$

Ⓓ $\frac{18}{100}$

9 An airline employs 10,208 people. Add the missing number to show another way to write 10,208.

10,000 + _______ + 8

10 There are 365 days in a year and 24 hours in a day. How many hours are there in a year?

Ⓐ 8,540

Ⓑ 8,560

Ⓒ 8,740

Ⓓ 8,760

11 Which number comes next in the pattern below?

85, 77, 69, 61, 53, …

Write your answer on the line below.

____

12 A rectangular field has a length of 80 metres and a width of 40 metres. What is the perimeter of the field? Write your answer on the line below.

____________ metres

13 A play sold $98 worth of tickets. Each ticket cost the same amount.

Which of these could be the cost of each ticket?

Ⓐ $6

Ⓑ $8

Ⓒ $12

Ⓓ $14

14 What is the rule to find the value of a term in the sequence below?

Position, *n*	**Value of Term**
1	3
2	5
3	7
4	9

Ⓐ $4n - 4$

Ⓑ $3n$

Ⓒ $2n + 1$

Ⓓ $n + 2$

15 The table below shows the number of households in three different suburbs.

Suburb	Number of Households
Wellington	135,682
Ashton	179,441
Ellis	120,597

Which is the best estimate of the total number of households in the three suburbs, to the nearest ten thousand?

Ⓐ 400,000

Ⓑ 435,720

Ⓒ 436,000

Ⓓ 440,000

16 Annabelle's flight to Canberra leaves at 13:30. Which of these also gives the time the flight leaves?

Ⓐ 1:30 a.m.

Ⓑ 1:30 p.m.

Ⓒ 3:30 a.m.

Ⓓ 3:30 p.m.

17 How is the numeral 9.007 written in words?

Ⓐ Nine and seven tenths

Ⓑ Nine and seven thousandths

Ⓒ Nine and seven hundredths

Ⓓ Nine thousand and seven

18 The table below shows the shirt number of four players on a basketball team.

Player	Shirt Number
Don	12
Jamie	17
Curtis	22
Chan	9

Which player has a multiple of 6 for a shirt number?

Ⓐ Don

Ⓑ Jamie

Ⓒ Curtis

Ⓓ Chan

19 Ursula plotted the point (8, 6) on a coordinate grid. She then added a second point 2 units to the left of the first point and 3 units down. What are the coordinates of the second point?

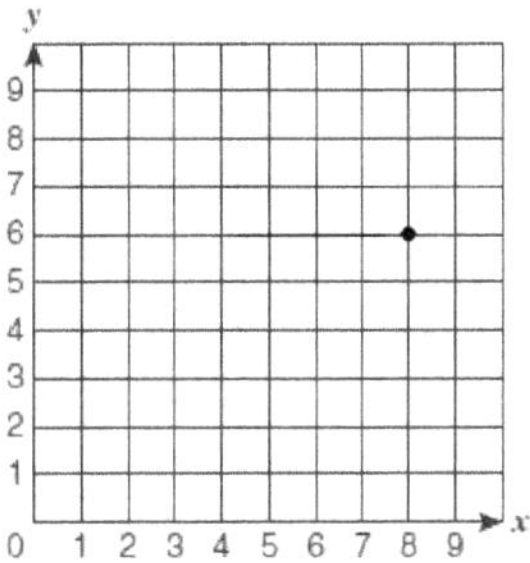

Ⓐ (6, 3)

Ⓑ (6, 9)

Ⓒ (10, 3)

Ⓓ (10, 9)

20 A juice bar sells 3 sizes of drinks. The table shows the number of drinks of each size sold in one day.

Size	Amount
Small	162
Medium	257
Large	188

Which of these is the closest estimate of how many more medium drinks the juice bar sold than small drinks?

Ⓐ 70

Ⓑ 80

Ⓒ 90

Ⓓ 100

21 The model below is made up of 1-centimetre cubes. What is the volume of the model?

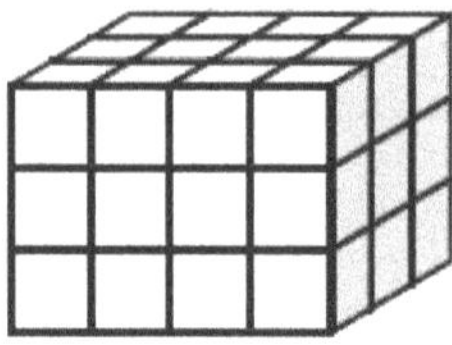

Write your answer on the line below.

___________ cubic centimetres

22 Miranda has the cardboard shapes shown below. Which of these could Miranda make using all three shapes?

Ⓐ Cone

Ⓑ Sphere

Ⓒ Rectangular prism

Ⓓ Cylinder

23 An Italian restaurant sells four types of meals. The owner made this graph to show how many meals of each type were sold one night.

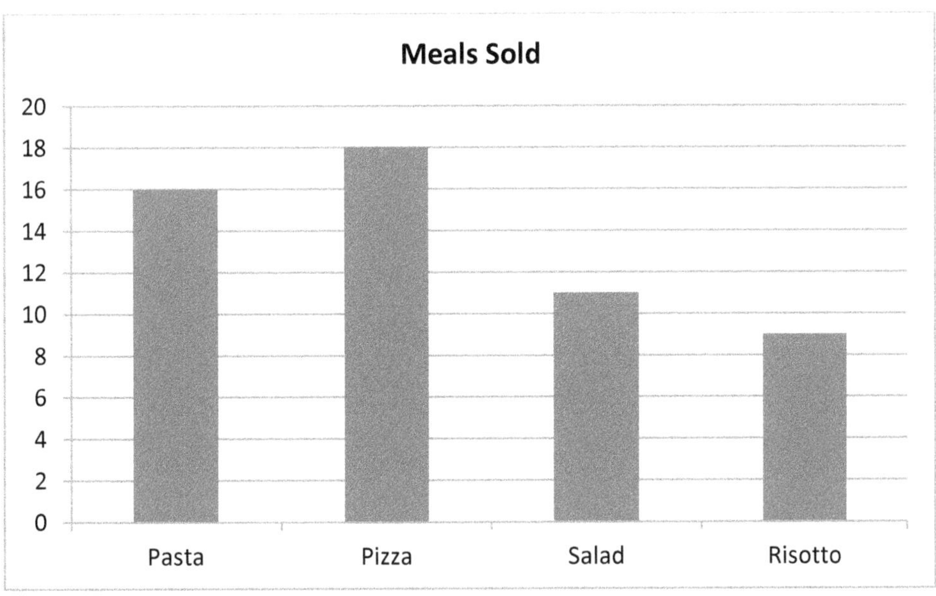

According to the graph, which statement is true?

Ⓐ The store sold more pizza meals than salad and risotto meals combined.

Ⓑ The store sold twice as many pizza meals as risotto meals.

Ⓒ The store sold more pasta meals than any other type of meal.

Ⓓ The store sold half as many salad meals as pasta meals.

24 At the start of the week, a plant had a height of $\frac{5}{8}$ inches. The plant grew $\frac{1}{4}$ of an inch during the week. Which diagram is shaded to show the height of the plant at the end of the week?

Ⓐ 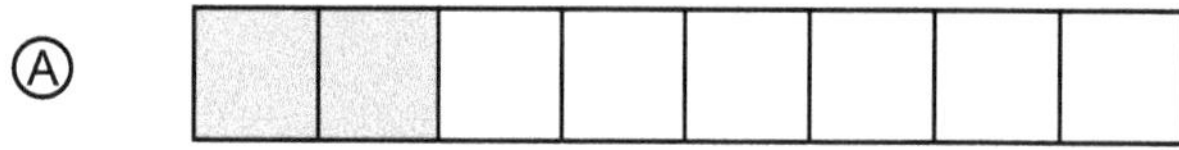

Ⓑ 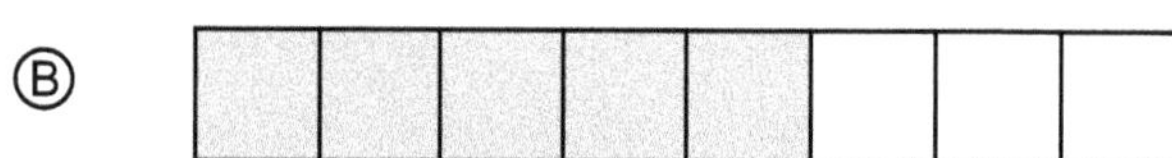

Ⓒ 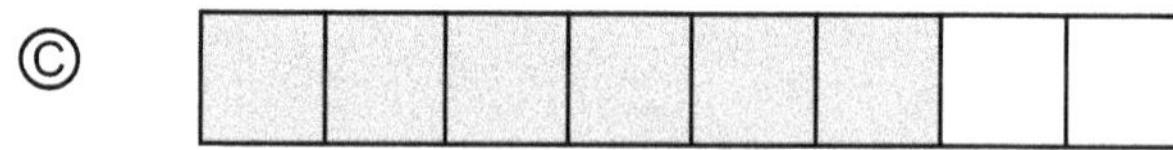

Ⓓ

25 How many millimetres are equivalent to 600 centimetres?

Ⓐ 0.6 mm

Ⓑ 6 mm

Ⓒ 60 mm

Ⓓ 6,000 mm

26 The grid below represents a garden.

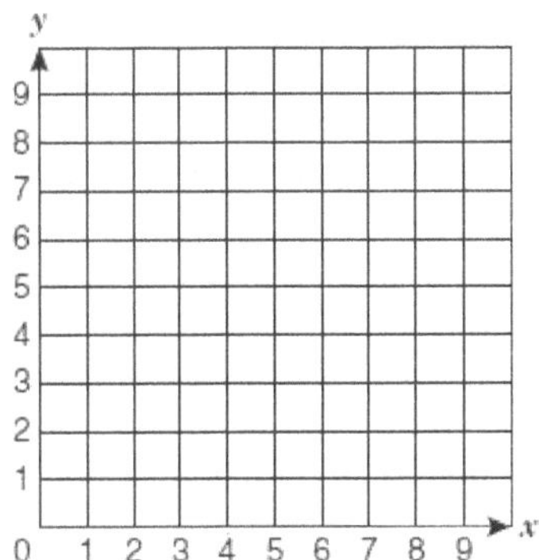

A lemon tree is located at the point (5, 4). An orange tree is located 4 units to the left of the lemon tree. Which ordered pair represents the location of the orange tree?

Ⓐ (9, 4)

Ⓑ (1, 4)

Ⓒ (5, 9)

Ⓓ (5, 0)

27 Which single transformation is shown below?

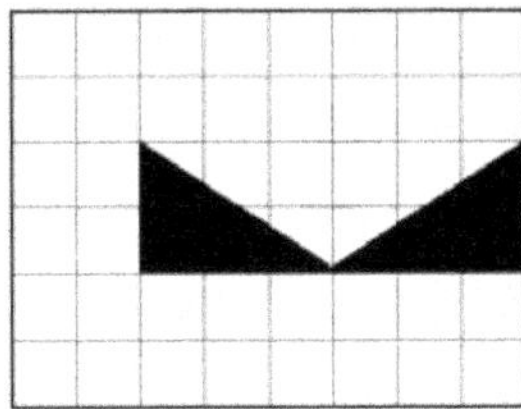

Ⓐ Translation

Ⓑ Reflection

Ⓒ Rotation

Ⓓ Dilation

28 Harris saved \$156 in 26 weeks. He saved the same amount of money each week. How much money did Harris save each week? Write your answer on the line below.

\$ ____________________

29 The table shows the side length of an equilateral triangle and the perimeter of an equilateral triangle.

Side Length, *l* (inches)	**Perimeter, *P* (inches)**
2	6
3	9
4	12
5	15

Which equation represents the relationship between side length and perimeter?

Ⓐ $P = l + 4$

Ⓑ $P = 3l$

Ⓒ $l = P + 4$

Ⓓ $l = 3P$

30 Sasha has 11 green blocks, 3 red blocks, 2 yellow blocks, and 4 blue blocks in a container. If she draws a block at random from the container, what is the probability that she will draw a yellow block?

Ⓐ $\frac{1}{5}$

Ⓑ $\frac{1}{10}$

Ⓒ $\frac{1}{4}$

Ⓓ $\frac{1}{8}$

31 What do the shaded models below show?

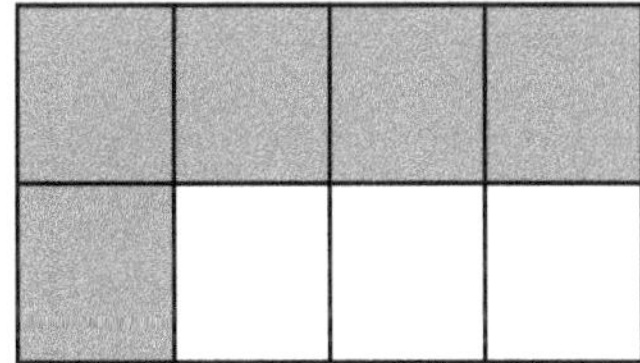

Ⓐ $\frac{5}{8} > \frac{1}{2}$

Ⓑ $\frac{5}{8} = \frac{1}{2}$

Ⓒ $\frac{5}{8} < \frac{4}{8}$

Ⓓ $\frac{5}{8} > \frac{1}{5}$

32 Which number is a factor of 57?

Ⓐ 11

Ⓑ 13

Ⓒ 17

Ⓓ 19

33 The table below shows the total cost of hiring DVDs for different numbers of DVDs.

Number of DVDs	Total Cost
2	$6
5	$15
6	$18
8	$24

What is the relationship between the number of DVDs hired and the total cost in dollars?

Ⓐ The total cost is 3 times the number of DVDs.

Ⓑ The total cost is 6 times the number of DVDs.

Ⓒ The total cost is 4 more than the number of DVDs.

Ⓓ The total cost is 10 more than the number of DVDs.

34 The picture below represents a floor rug.

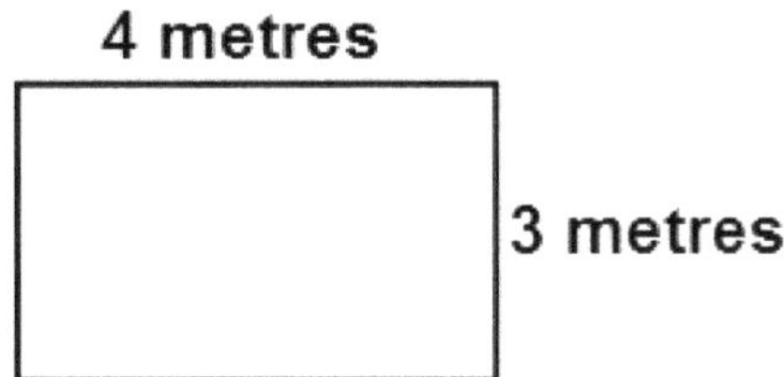

What is the perimeter of the floor rug? Write your answer on the line below.

____________________ metres

35 Mr. Singh bought 2 adult zoo tickets for a total of $22, as well as 4 children's tickets. He spent $54 in total. How much was each children's ticket?

Ⓐ $8

Ⓑ $2.50

Ⓒ $9

Ⓓ $13.50

36 Joanne had three singing lessons one week. Two lessons went for 45 minutes, and one lesson went for 60 minutes. Which number sentence could be used to find how many minutes Joanne had singing lessons for?

Ⓐ (2 x 45) x 60

Ⓑ (2 + 45) x 60

Ⓒ (2 x 45) + 60

Ⓓ (2 + 45) + 60

37 Jason used cubes to make the model shown below. What is the volume of the model?

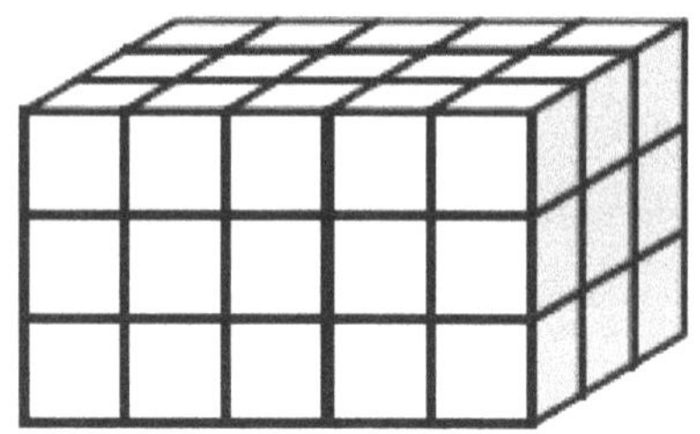

Ⓐ 15 cubic units

Ⓑ 45 cubic units

Ⓒ 50 cubic units

Ⓓ 75 cubic units

38 What is the measure of the angle shown below?

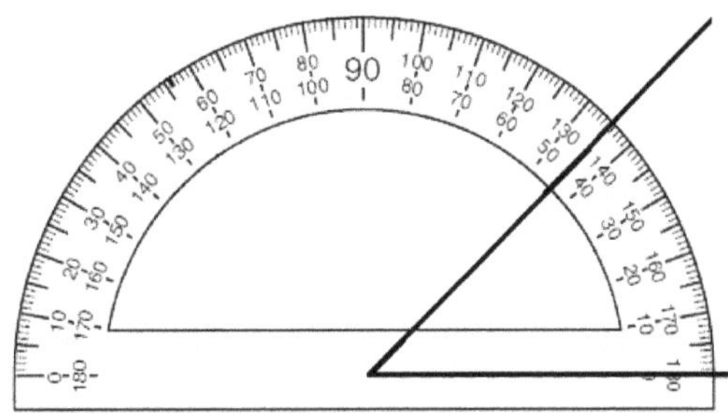

Write your answer on the line below.

________________ °

39 Emily cooked a roast on high for $1\frac{1}{4}$ hours. She then cooked it for another $\frac{1}{2}$ hour on low. How many minutes did she cook the roast for in all?

Ⓐ 75 minutes

Ⓑ 90 minutes

Ⓒ 105 minutes

Ⓓ 120 minutes

40 The dot plot below shows the number of athletics events entered by each student in a class.

Number of Athletics Events Entered

	X			
X	X		X	
X	X		X	X
X	X	X	X	X
X	X	X	X	X
X	X	X	X	X
1	2	3	4	5

How many students entered 4 or more events? Write your answer on the line below.

____

END OF PRACTICE TEST

ANSWER KEY

Practice Set 1

1. 7	2. D	3. C	4. C	5. 2
6. B	7. D	8. 24	9. D	10. B
11. C	12. D	13. D	14. 96	15. A
16. C	17. 680	18. D	19. A	20. B

Practice Set 2

1. $532	2. C	3. A	4. B	5. 24
6. C	7. 2,400	8. B	9. A	10. C
11. A	12. C	13. A	14. B	15. B
16. A	17. 28	18. C	19. 44	20. B

Practice Set 3

1. 22	2. A	3. D	4. D	5. B
6. D	7. 13	8. C	9. A	10. 183
11. A	12. A	13. C	14. C	15. A
16. D	17. B	18. 120	19. D	20. C

Practice Test 1

1. C	2. 33	3. B	4. 718	5. 64
6. C	7. B	8. B	9. C	10. B
11. C	12. B	13. B	14. A	15. D
16. 26	17. D	18. 8	19. C	20. D
21. C	22. C	23. C	24. C	25. C
26. D	27. $14	28. A	29. B	30. A
31. D	32. D	33. 6	34. C	35. B
36. C	37. B	38. D	39. 12,381	40. D

Practice Test 2

1. D	2. 105	3. C	4. D	5. C
6. 43	7. C	8. D	9. B	10. C
11. D	12. 6	13. B	14. B	15. A
16. 98	17. 63	18. D	19. C	20. D
21. 8	22. B	23. D	24. B	25. A
26. D	27. B	28. 55.1	29. B	30. B
31. 65°	32. C	33. D	34. C	35. C
36. D	37. B	38. A	39. D	40. 135

Practice Test 3

1. D	2. A	3. B	4. 12	5. B
6. C	7. C	8. A	9. 200	10. D
11. 45	12. 240	13. D	14. C	15. D
16. B	17. B	18. A	19. A	20. D
21. 36	22. D	23. B	24. D	25. C
26. B	27. B	28. $6	29. B	30. B
31. A	32. D	33. A	34. 14	35. A
36. C	37. B	38. 45°	39. C	40. 9

www.ingramcontent.com/pod-product-compliance
Ingram Content Group Australia Pty Ltd
76 Discovery Rd, Dandenong South VIC 3175, AU
AUHW011405020126
421644AU00013B/501

9 781925 783193